Volume Two
Later Elementary

Accent on GILLOCK

by William Gillock

CONTENTS

ISBN 978-0-87718-077-7

EXCLUSIVELY DISTRIBUTED BY

Visit Hal Leonard Online at
www.halleonard.com

Contact us:
Hal Leonard
7777 West Bluemound Road
Milwaukee, WI 53213
Email: info@halleonard.com

In Europe, contact:
Hal Leonard Europe Limited
42 Wigmore Street
Marylebone, London, W1U 2RN
Email: info@halleonardeurope.com

In Australia, contact:
Hal Leonard Australia Pty. Ltd.
4 Lentara Court
Cheltenham, Victoria, 3192 Australia
Email: info@halleonard.com.au

The Glass Slipper

William Gillock

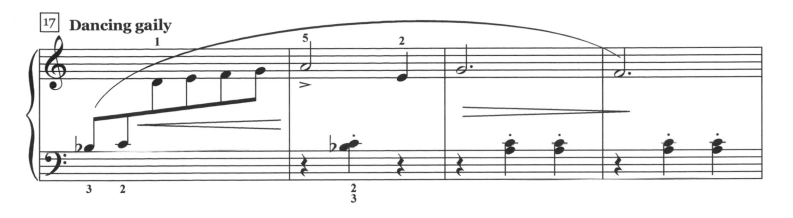

Dancing gaily

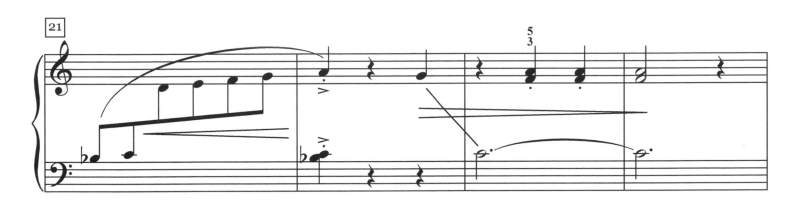

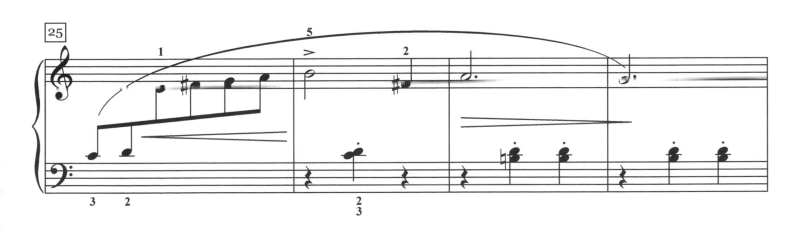

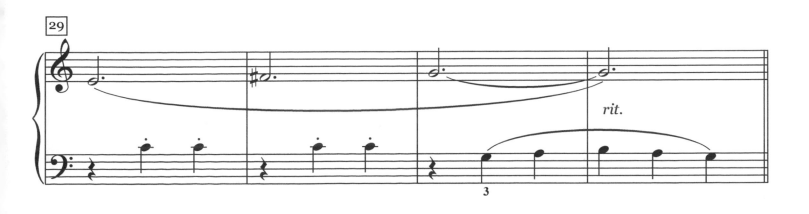

rit.

4

33 **As at first**

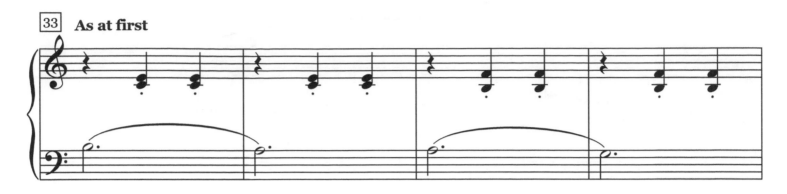

37

42

Cinderella runs away...

46

L.H.

...losing her slipper!

Clowns

William Gillock

French Doll

William Gillock

Delicately; gracefully

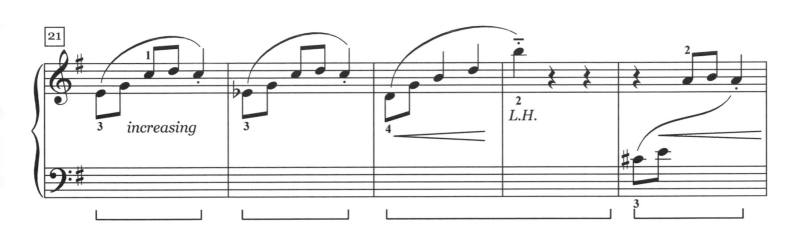

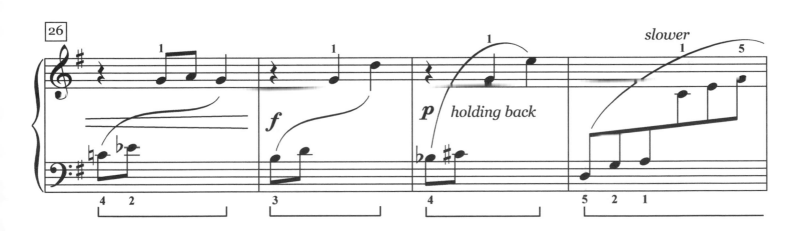

Moonlight

Up-stems R.H.
Down-stems L.H.

William Gillock

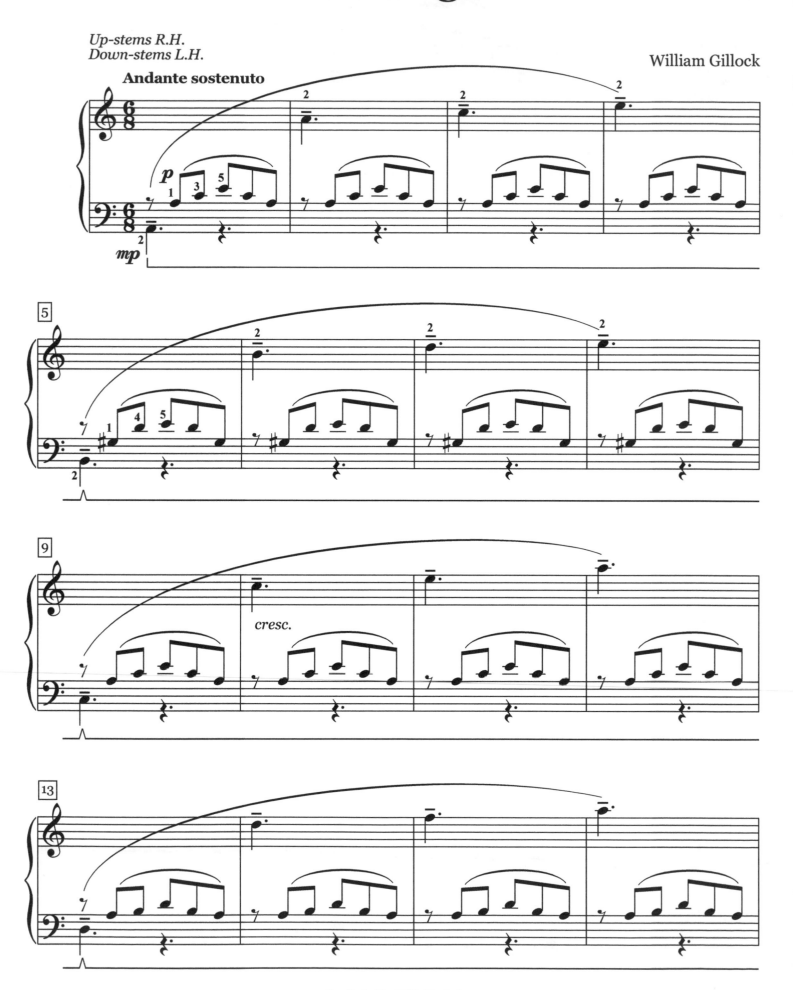

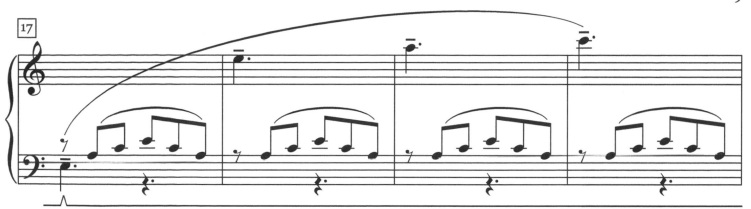

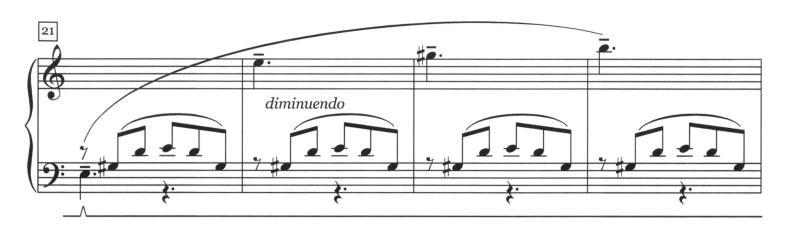

German Dance
Op. 17, No.9

Ludwig van Beethoven
(1770–1827)
Arranged by William Gillock

Lively waltz tempo

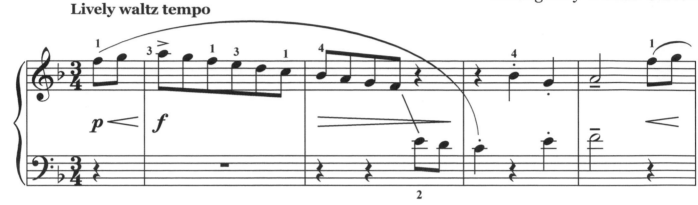

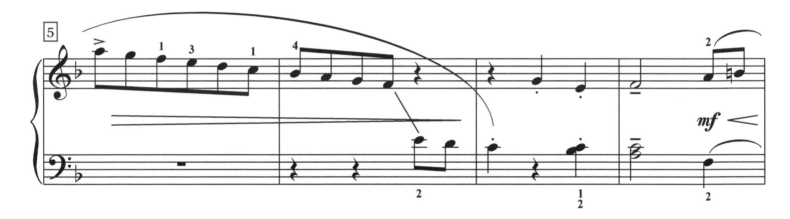

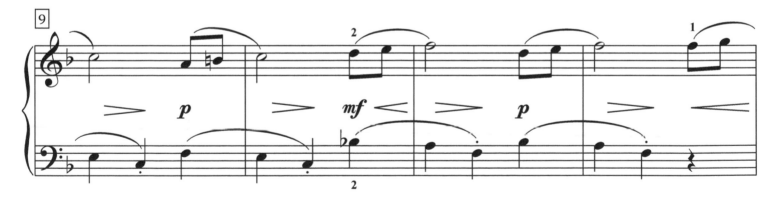

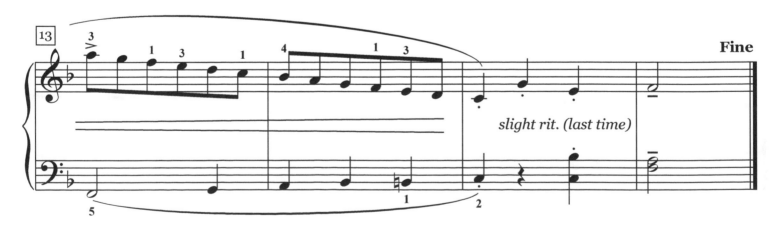

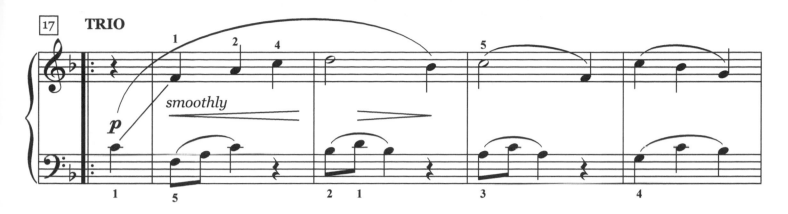

The Haunted Tree

William Gillock

To Sister M. Leola

Mission Bells

William Gillock

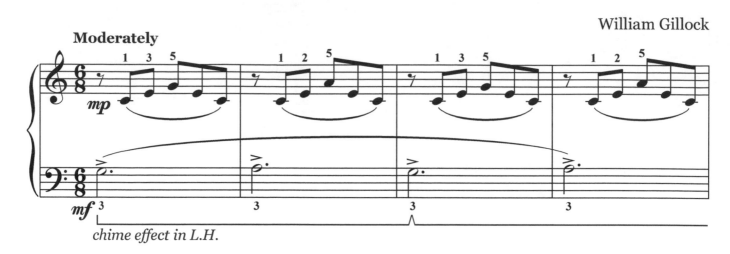

chime effect in L.H.

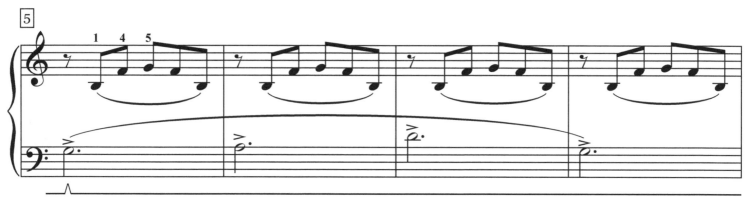

R.H. slurs simile

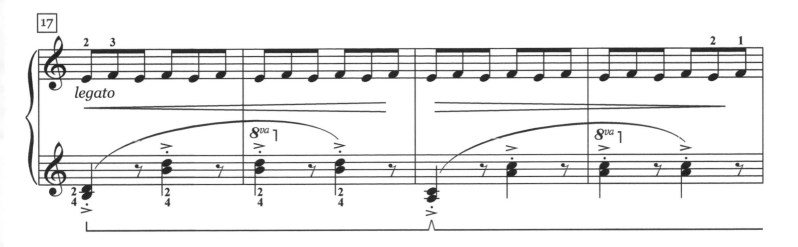

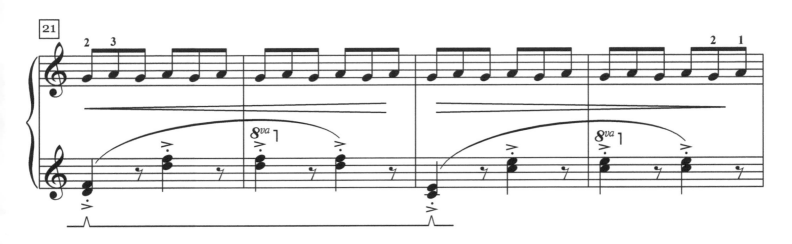

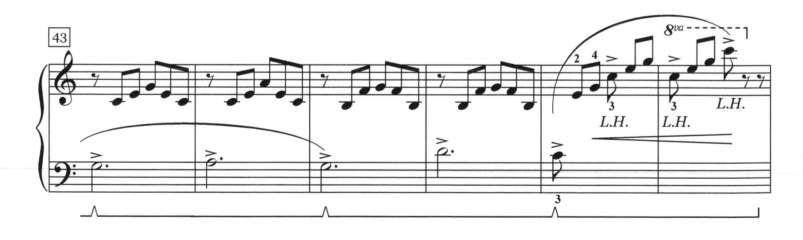

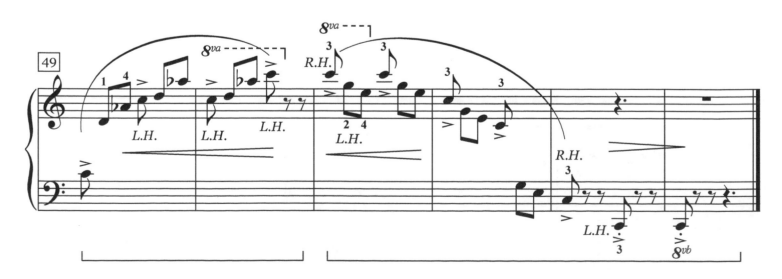